SUMMER 2018

IN THIS ISSUE:

[COMING THIS FALL]

[**FALL**CENTRAL REPORT]

FROM THE EDITORS:

Every season is beautiful in the Hudson Valley. Summer is a perfect time to build, create and execute visions that were born earlier this year. In this issue we are ascending above the Valley and introducing our globally-oriented Landida and ToughConstruct Brands, as well as few other news from the Duncan Avenue Group.

Maxwell Alexander & Dino Alexander

It's your home's focal point. The site of some of your best moments and the base of operations for entertaining - it's your kitchen, and no room in your home is more valuable. A magnificent kitchen defines a home, and bringing your kitchen to this level means capitalizing on today's top trends.

Many of the trends that will define kitchens for the year appear first at KBIS, the kitchen and bath industry convention held every year in January. More than 600 brands attended this year's event, and here are the five trends that stood out from the show and are sure to dictate kitchen styles for the rest of this year and beyond.

APPLIANCES THAT CAN DO IT ALL

As home chefs have become much more refined, the need for kitchen appliances capable of delivering to these expectations has increased. Signature Kitchen Suite, the new-to-the-scene luxury brand, for example, debuted the first-of-its-kind pro-style range with built-in sous vide for the ultimate in precision cooking. The range is among the most versatile available with two extra-high burners that deliver 23,000 BTUs of cooking power and two ultra-low burners to maintain temperatures as low as 100 degrees. This appliance is also Wi-Fi enabled, which means you can monitor and control your kitchen wherever you are.

UNIQUE BACKSPLASHES

The tile backsplash still has plenty of staying power, but the latest trends are upping the wow factor of this kitchen mainstay. From mirrored glass and backlit onyx to decorative sculptures, the kitchen backsplash is becoming the statement piece of any kitchen and a unique way to express your own style and taste.

5 TOP TRENDS FOR YOUR KITCHEN DESIGN

(BPT)

MATTE BLACK FINISHES

The standard appearance of kitchen fixtures is taking on a darker tone in 2018, as matte black finishes are flourishing in a big way. This elegant, luxe appliance finish complements any kitchen and is also designed to conceal fingerprints and smudges. This smooth, low-gloss design option enhances any style kitchen, from modern to farmhouse, traditional to contemporary and every style in between.

DESIGN ELEMENTS

Long a place of functional purity, the kitchen is getting a dramatically artistic makeover in 2018. Designers from one side of KBIS to the other were showcasing lavish kitchens complemented with unique patterns, angles and texture choices. You simply wanted to go out and touch and savor every single detail they offered. The takeaway? It is possible to enjoy looking at your kitchen as much as you enjoy working in it.

SMARTER KITCHENS

New Wi-Fi enabled appliances are helping people control their homes in new ways, allowing for greater convenience - either through the touch of a button on their smartphone or via voice commands through Amazon Alexa and Google Assistant. Want to preheat the oven before you head home from work? Done! Need a fresh batch of ice before company arrives? You don't even have to get up. Forget to turn on the dishwasher? No problem. Choose a cycle and turn it on from virtually anywhere. Smart home leaders like LG have also teamed with food and recipe services such as Innit and SideChef to better assist home chefs with planning, shopping, preparing and cooking delicious meals.

Taking your kitchen to the next level The latest and greatest innovations for your kitchen were on display at KBIS, but bringing them home is up to you. Need more renovation inspiration? Check out new virtual design tools to experiment with different styles and appliance combinations to create your dream kitchen. You may just find a whole new look for your kitchen.

DA
AROMATHERAPY™
SOOTHING
AROMATHERAPY
MIST
with
EUCALYPTUS
& PEPPERMINT
ESSENTIAL OILS
2 FL. OZ. // 59 ML.
DA
CALMING
AROMATHERAPY
MIST
with
LAVENDER
& CHAMOMILE
ESSENTIAL OILS
2 FL. OZ. // 59 ML.

SCROLL LESS. BREATHE DEEPER.
DA-AROMATHERAPY.COM

[ASCENDING ABOVE THE VALLEY]

Photo Essay by **Maxwell Alexander**

ASCENDING ABOVE
A MYSTERY
ON THE HUDSON
CORNWALL ON HUDSON, NY

Photo Essay by **Maxwell Alexander**

ASCENDING ABOVE
MAHICANNITUCK
THE SLEEPING GIANT
NEWBURGH, NY

ASCENDING ABOVE STORMKING

CORNWALL, NY

Photo Essay by **Maxwell Alexander**

[ASCENDING ABOVE THE VALLEY]

Photo Essay by **Maxwell Alexander**

ASCENDING ABOVE [A MYSTERY ON THE HUDSON

CORNWALL ON HUDSON, NY

[HUDSONVALLEY.STYLE]

[HUDSON VALLEY STYLE GETAWAY]

LAMBS
HILL

BEACON/NY

Photo Story
by Maxwell Alexander

LAMBS HILL - BEACON/NY

Charlotte Guernsey (Lambs Hill Venue Designer & Owner)
+ Equestrian Suite Resident **Lukka**

AN
EXPERIENCE
STEEPED
IN HISTORY
& HIGH-END
DESIGN
Mylen
PEEKSKILL
NEW YORK

LambsHill
Venue | Bridal Boutique | Design

MODERN
AUTHENTIC
RUSTIC

WAKE UP TO HUDSON VALLEY

LAMBS HILL // EQUESTRIAN SUITE

ONCE IN A LIFETIME

LAMBSHILL.COM

STOP THE MOWING MADNESS WITH AN ECO-FRIENDLY LANDIDA™ ROCK LAWN

*by **Maxwell Alexander, CEO & Founder of Landida™ — Smart Landscapes***

While a thick carpet of grass is, unfortunately, the most common lawn option, many homeowners in the United States and all around the World are drawn to the appeal of maintenance-free rock lawns. These pebble-based ground coverings are ideal for regions that are under watering restrictions due to drought (which is basically the entire Planet earth), or for homeowners who are just tired of constant mowing and inhaling pesticides/herbicides that come with their grass lawn. The installation process is similar to installing mulch or rock in a flower bed but encompasses the entire lawn instead. A rock lawn requires almost no ongoing maintenance and actually draws attention to the low-maintenance, evergreen shrubs and trees. In addition, Landida™ Smart Landscapes rock lawns look equally good in the winter as they do in the summer.

LANDIDA™ SMART LANDSCAPES / ROCK LAWN BENEFITS

Eliminating the grass from a lawn may seem like a drastic move, but it actually has many time saving and eco-friendly benefits.

- Reduces the amount of time required to mow, water and fertilize grass.

- Conserves water by eliminating the need to water the lawn.

- Reduces or completely eliminates pesticides applied to the lawn.

- Reduces the amount of yard waste, such as grass, leaves and pine needles, that is sent to the landfill.

- Some cities located in drought-prone areas of the Southwest even provide tax breaks for homeowners who replace their lawn with rock or gravel. This incentive strives to conserve as much water as possible for human consumption.

WHAT TO EXPECT WHEN INSTALLING LANDIDA™ SMART LANDSCAPES

We will measure the width and length of the lawn, and multiply the two numbers together to arrive at the square footage of the lawn. We will determine how many tons of rock you need by dividing the number by 100 for 1-inch diameter rock or by 110 for 1/2-inch diameter rock. These measurements are for the recommended installation depth of 2 inches.

AMERICA
IS CONVERTING
TO INTELLIGENT
LANDSCAPES

are you?

landida™
SMART LANDSCAPES

INTELLIGENT WATER-CONSERVING LANDSCAPE ™

PESTICIDE / HERBICIDE FREE LANDSCAPE ™

TURF GRASS / MAINTENANCE-FREE LANDSCAPE ™

PET FRIENDLY LANDSCAPE • BUGS & DIRT FREE ™

CLIMATE CHANGE CONSCIOUS DESIGN ™

get grass-free at landida.com

MAXWELL
ALEXANDER | HOME™

LANDIDA™ PROFESSIONALS WILL PREPARE THE AREA

Landida™ Smart Landscapes experts will remove all grass and weeds from the area using a spade to slide under the top 1 to 2 inches of soil. We will place the material into a wheelbarrow and move it to a compost area preferably on your property or a certified compost site. We will not remove any trees or shrubs that you want to remain in place. Instead of spraying the ground with an herbicide, we will install black weed-barrier landscaping fabric.

INSTALLING THE LANDIDA™ ROCK LAWN

Landida™ Smart Landscapes Experts will spread the material out to an even 2-inch thickness using a bow rake. They will repeat the process of spreading out the rock until the entire surface of the lawn is covered. Although we can use any type of gravel or rock desired, river-run gravel is rounded and more comfortable to walk on for both humans and pets, and bluestone 3/8 gravel is just as comfortable to walk on plus has a stylish and sophisticated look. We will rinse the top of the rocks with a garden hose to remove any white residue.

No matter the motivation, Landida™ Smart Landscapes Rock Lawns are attractive landscaping options for all areas of the country. Not only do homeowners reduce the amount of money they spend on the lawn, they gain more time to enjoy their home instead of just maintaining it.

ENJOY YOUR YARD INSTEAD OF MOWING IT!

aglaïa

Recycled metal is as beautiful and timeless as newly mined and indistinguishable in its use as a raw material, Aglaia Jewelry made its choice, have you?

aglaiajewelry.com

AM
ALEXANDER
MAXWELL
REALTY
™

REAL ESTATE PHOTOGRAPHY 101

61% MORE VIEWS ONLINE WITH PROFESSIONAL PHOTOS

UP TO **47%** HIGHER ASKING PRICE/SQFT

80% OF BUYERS CITED THEY WOULDN'T EVEN CONSIDER A LISTING WITHOUT PHOTOGRAPHS

98% OF BUYERS THINK PROFESSIONAL PHOTOS ARE MOST USEFUL WHEN LOOKING FOR HOME ONLINE

AERIAL & DRONE IMAGING

CONSIDER THESE HIGH-TECH UPGRADES

DUNCANAVENUE™

HUDSON VALLEY REAL ESTATE SERVICES

SCHEDULE YOUR PHOTOSHOOT @

DUNCANAVENUE.COM

STATISTICS SOURCE:
NATIONAL ASSOCIATION OF REALTORS

PROFESSIONAL LIGHTING

DSLR CAMERAS & LENSES

PROFESSIONAL RETOUCHING

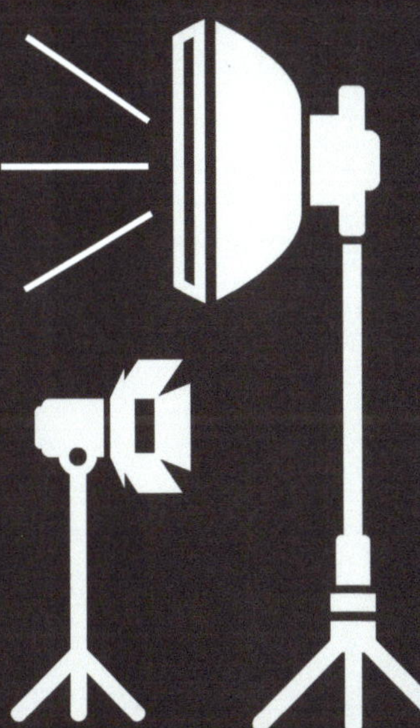

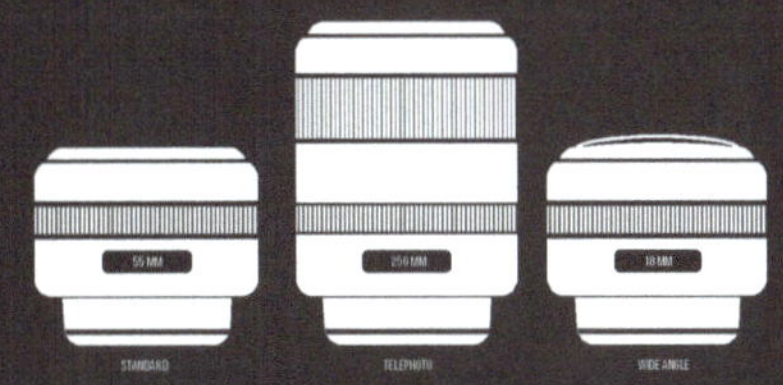

+ DIGITAL STAGING

COPAKE LAKE ESTATE

PHOTO STORY BY MAXWELL ALEXANDER

[HUDSON VALLEY STYLE PROPERTIES]

[OPEN]

[REFLECT]

[LIVE]

DA SKY™
AERIAL PHOTOGRAPHY
by
DUNCANAVENUE™
[DUNCANAVENUE.COM/SKY]

[EXPERIENCE THE MAGIC
OF HUDSON VALLEY]

[HUDSON VALLEY STYLE KITCHEN DESIGN]

HAVEN HOMES / CORNWALL, NY /
PHOTOGRAPHY BY MAXWELL ALEXANDER

[HUDSON VALLEY STYLE PROPERTIES]

HAVEN HOMES / CORNWALL, NY /
PHOTOGRAPHY BY MAXWELL ALEXANDER

3 ELEMENTS TO CREATE A DREAM BATHROOM SANCTUARY

(BPT) - Bathrooms reign supreme, overtaking kitchens as the most popular remodeling project, according to a new survey by the National Association of Home Builders. In the study, remodelers reported on the most common projects in 2017 and 81 percent performed bathroom remodeling.

Whether you're hiring the project out or taking the DIY route, fashioning the bathroom of your dreams can enhance your home's value and add enjoyment to your daily routine. A leading trend in bathroom design is to create a space that is not only functional but is a true sanctuary. To craft a spa-like bath setting that you'll love for years to come, consider these elements.

— 1 —
SINKS & VANITIES

"Clutter causes chaos that can add to daily stress. To establish a peaceful retreat without the disorder that commonly overtakes bathrooms, it's important to keep organization in mind when selecting a sink and vanity combination. The key is to find a balance between style and functionality.

Consider the DXV Modulus collection, which creates simple yet dramatic spaces with a selection of trending materials and finishes for optimum style. Its modular concept, highlighted with minimalistic bathroom sinks and coordinating vanities, allows for maximum flexibility in installation and organization. It brings high design to any project, including master bathrooms and powder rooms, where space may be at a premium.

A true spa-like bathroom environment can be created right at home, combining high-style bathroom fixtures with modular styling and discreet organizational features.

The DXV Modulus collection can help create your own bathroom sanctuary with its modular design, which offers maximum flexibility in organization. Luxurious options include a deep soaking freestanding tub.

— 2 —
FREESTANDING TUBS

When you select the right tub for your new bathroom, you're giving yourself a way to unwind every day, as well as provide a stunning focal point to anchor the space. Deep soak freestanding tubs are a top trend for the ultimate in bathing relaxation. Immersing yourself in the warm water of a soaking tub can help ease muscle tension, making you feel like you're at the spa while bathing in the comfort of your own home.

Soothing, romantic and indulgent, DXV soaking tubs create the perfect personal sanctuary. This must-have showstopper adds style, repose and a touch of luxury that elevates any bathroom setting.

— 3 —
SHOWER SYSTEMS

Forget boring single showerheads. Today's complete shower systems go beyond the basic clean to provide a comprehensive bathing experience. Design the space to fit your preferences with different sprays and various angles for massage, invigoration or total relaxation. You can adjust the flow and temperature to your liking. It's customization on demand.

To further enhance the shower experience, add in spa-like elements, like your choice of adjustable lighting and music to match your mood. Go ahead and close your eyes, feel the water, and escape while getting lost in your

With the right elements and well-thought-out design, you can craft your own personal oasis. Adding to your home's value while relishing in its pleasure - now that's a dream come true.

TO STAGE, OR NOT TO STAGE?

Learn More about this design project →
at duncanavenue.com/design

STAGED HOMES SELL 79% FASTER

STAGED HOMES SOLD IN 11 DAYS OR LESS

ON AVERAGE SPEND **73%** LESS TIME ON THE MARKET

81% OF BUYERS

FIND THAT STAGING HELPS THEM BETTER **VISUALIZE A PROPERTY AS THEIR FUTURE HOME**

HIGHER SALES PRICES

STAGED HOMES SELL FOR **17% MORE** THAN NON-STAGED HOMES

BUYERS MOST OFTEN offer 1%-5% increase on the REAL VALUE OF A STAGED HOME

SELLERS SPEND LESS THAN 1% FOR STAGING SERVICES

to get a **1000% RETURN ON INVESTMENT**

HOME STAGING CAN BOOST PERCEIVED VALUE OF A HOME BY 20%

95% OF BUYER'S AGENTS SAY THAT HOME STAGING HAS A POSITIVE EFFECT ON THE HOME BUYER'S VIEW OF THE PROPERTY

3% YET LESS THAN 3% OF HOMES LISTED ON MLS ARE STAGED

DA SKY™
AERIAL PHOTOGRAPHY
by
DUNCANAVENUE™
[DUNCANAVENUE.COM]

HAVING YOUR HOME PROFESSIONALLY PHOTOGRAPHED?

by **Maxwell Alexander,** President, Chief Design Officer, Duncan Avenue Group

The real estate market in the Hudson Valley and around the Globe has been changing rapidly, and that has created some challenges for home sellers. It was not that long ago that searching for a home meant driving from New York City all the way to beautiful Hudson Valley neighborhoods, picking up flyers and sales packets and maybe stumbling upon on open house or two.

In the 21st century, home searches are more likely to start online while at lunch break in the office than in the family car. The ease of browsing real estate listings online is hard to beat, and potential buyers can scour dozens of listings in the time it would take to visit just one in person.

The shift to online home shopping has created both challenges and opportunities. If you understand how home buyers shop and what they are looking for, then you can make your listing stand out and rise above the rest. If you fail to put your home in its best light, would-be buyers could pass your home by as they do their online shopping.

Hiring a local Hudson Valley professional photographer is one of the best ways to make your home stand out. Duncan Avenue Real Estate Photography Studio is your premier professional photography provider in the Hudson Valley area including Orange, Rockland, Dutchess, Ulster, Putnam, Westchester, Greene, Rensselaer, Columbia, Saratoga and Albany Counties. We'll take care of making your online photographs stand out, but there are certain things you should do before the pro arrives. Here are the steps you should take while you wait for the photographer.

SECURE YOUR PETS

If you have a dog that is aggressive, territorial or just protective, be sure to secure the animal long before the photographer is scheduled to arrive. We love dogs, and in fact we've got two super hyper Jack Russell Terriers at home, however they could definitely get in a way of making your home look good in the pictures, especially if they are so cute that it's just way too distracting.

Even if your pets are not too aggressive, they could get in the way during the photo shoot. Placing your cats and dogs in the basement or garage is a courtesy you should extend to the professional who will be photographing your home.

START A FIRE

If your home has a fireplace, we would want to show it off. Be sure you have a roaring fire going in each of your fireplaces before the

HERE IS WHAT TO DO BEFORE THE PHOTOGRAPHER ARRIVES

photographer arrives.

A lit fireplace will not only make your home look inviting, but it also serves as proof that it's working correctly. A fireplace can be a big selling point, so do not sell yourself short.

| LIGHT SOME CANDLES

You can create a homey and inviting environment even if your home does not have a fireplace. Just pick your favorite candles, scatter them around the house and light them up when the photographer arrives.

A set of tapers on the table will create a romantic setting and make your finished photographs look great. A large pillar candle in the living room will create an inviting atmosphere and encourage browsers to take a look. Use your imagination, and ask your Hudson Valley Real Estate Photography Pro for other lighting ideas when he arrives.

| LIGHT IT UP

Speaking of lighting, turn all the lights on before the photographer's scheduled arrival. If any light bulbs are burned out, take the time to replace them. Set the dimmers to full power so that your home looks as bright and airy as possible.

You can let even more light in by rolling up the blinds and opening up the curtains. You want the space to be as bright and inviting as possible, and that brightness will come through in the finished photographs.

We will bring supplemental lighting with us to make sure all areas of your home look the best they can.

| CLEAR OUT THE DRIVEWAY

We would want shots of the driveway, so remove any cars, trucks or other vehicles before the scheduled photo shoot. Be sure to park them well down the street, keeping the road in front

of your home open as possible. Duncan Avenue Photography Studio is the only Real Estate Photography Studio that offers complementary FAA-licensed aerial/drone photography with every property or listing package.

Staging your home for open houses and private showings is important, but making your home look great in the listing photographs may be even more important. You can think of your listing photographs as a special kind of staging, one designed to draw the eyes of would-be buyers and get them to schedule a private appointment.

Make your appointment today at DuncanAvenue.com

Sara Golden